C1 Writing

Cambridge Masterclass

Margaret Cooze

© Prosperity Education Ltd. 2023

Registered offices: Sherlock Close, Cambridge
CB3 0HP, United Kingdom

First published 2023

ISBN: 978-1-913825-81-2

This publication is in copyright. Subject to statutory exception
and to the provisions of relevant collective licensing agreements,
no reproduction of any part may take place without the written
permission of Prosperity Education.

The moral right of the author has been asserted.

'Cambridge C1 Advanced' and 'CAE' are brands
belonging to The Chancellor, Masters and Scholars of the
University of Cambridge and are not associated with
Prosperity Education or its products.

Designed by ORP Cambridge

For further information and resources, visit:
www.prosperityeducation.net

To infinity and beyond.

Contents

Introduction	5
Task type **1. Essay**	17
Task type **2. Email**	25
Task type **3. Letter**	33
Task type **4. Proposal**	41
Task type **5. Report**	49
Task type **6. Review**	57
Practice tests	65

Margaret Cooze holds an MA in Applied Linguistics and an MSc in English Language Teaching Management, and has worked in senior roles at Cambridge English Language Assessment and Cambridge Assessment International Education. She is the author of several ELT resources published by Cambridge University Press.

Introduction

Cambridge C1 Advanced Writing

Welcome to this book on the Cambridge C1 Advanced Writing paper. C1 Advanced is one of the exams in the series provided by Cambridge Assessment – part of the University of Cambridge. It is the fourth in the range of tests they provide in General English:

A2	Key (KET)
B1	Preliminary (PET)
B2	First (FCE)
C1	Advanced (CAE)
C2	Proficiency (CPE)

The references next to each test refer to the CEFR Level (Common European Framework of Reference), and show the language level of each test.

For CEFR C1 Writing, you will be able to:

- communicate complex ideas effectively on a range of topics

- write clearly using a variety of cohesive devices and organisational patterns

- explain your viewpoint and communicate complex ideas effectively

- recognise the reader of texts, and use a consistently suitable register

- use a good range of simple and more complex grammatical structures with flexibility and control

- use a good range of vocabulary, including less common lexis, correctly and with precision

- recognise the functional language needed, and select language to convey meaning effectively.

How does the test work?

You can take the C1 Advanced exam on a computer or on paper. The content is the same for both forms of the test. The C1 Advanced Writing paper gives you the opportunity to show your language skills. The topics of tasks are chosen so that they are relevant to the typical student taking this exam, so you should find that you have enough ideas to write about. Each question will guide you by identifying the context, the purpose for writing and the target reader. It is important to remember that you aren't being tested on the subject content of the tasks. So, if the topic of the Part 1 question, for example, is voluntary work, you aren't expected to be an expert about this topic. The test format is:

Time allowed	1 hour and 30 minutes
Number of parts	2
Number of questions	Part 1: one compulsory question Part 2: one optional question from a choice of three
Task types	essay, letter, email, proposal, report, review
Length	each answer should be 220–260 words long

Task type 1: Essay

Part 1 (Question 1) of the Writing paper is always an essay written for your teacher; the format of the question is always the same and consists of three sections. Firstly, the topic and explanation are stated. The topic is based on an academic activity, such as taking part in a seminar or discussion. This is followed by three bullet points relating to the topic, and then three short comments related to the bullet points:

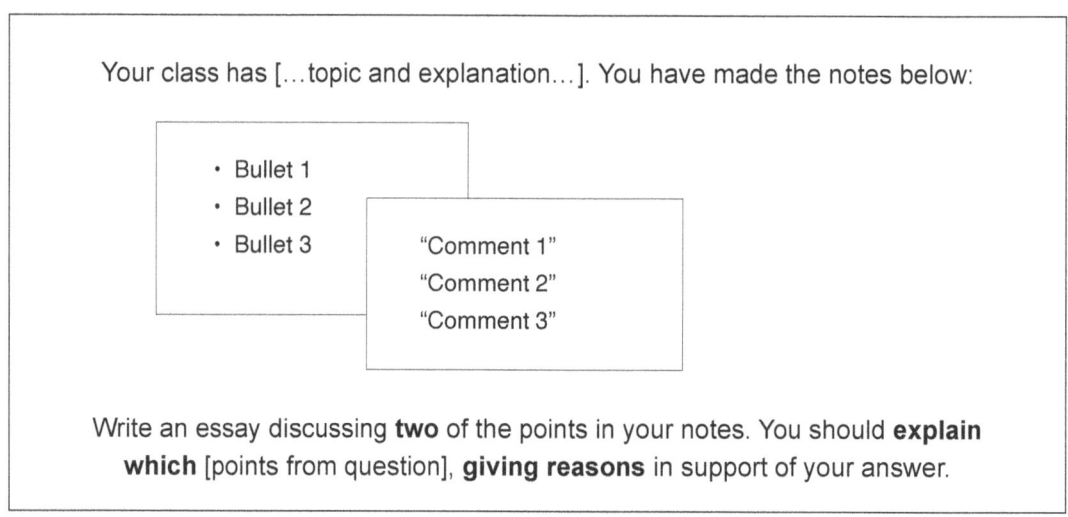

Your class has [...topic and explanation...]. You have made the notes below:

- Bullet 1
- Bullet 2
- Bullet 3

"Comment 1"
"Comment 2"
"Comment 3"

Write an essay discussing **two** of the points in your notes. You should **explain which** [points from question], **giving reasons** in support of your answer.

The emboldened words in the question provide a focus for your answer.

- You must cover **two** of the ideas in the bullet points (but you can say whether you agree or disagree with them) or, alternatively, you can discuss both sides.

- You must come to a decision to address the question prompted by the 'which' in the instructions.

- You must support your answer with **reasons**.

You can also add your own opinions. To complete the task you must include two points from the question, however, so make sure that you don't forget this if you also include your own ideas. The purpose of the essay is to allow you to show that you can select relevant information and can back this up with a supporting argument. Remember, you don't have to tell the truth! The examiners won't know, so if you don't have experience or an opinion you can make something up.

Your essay should be well-structured with clear and appropriate organisational features. Suitable introductions and conclusions should be included, and the structure of the essay and its paragraphing should guide the reader through the content, helping them understand the argument. Essays are written in a semi-formal register as you are writing for your teacher.

Task types 2 and 3: Letter/email

You may have the option of writing an email or letter in the C1 Advanced Writing paper. The two task types are very similar in that they require you to respond to a prompt or message given in the question. You don't need to worry too much about the layout – you won't be tested on whether the email has a 'To/From' line, for example. However, you should think about how to open your email or letter and what opening salutation and closing to use.

At C1, emails or letters are not limited to just giving information but will also require you to show some other functional language – for example, complaining or justifying a course of action. Your email or letter may be addressed to the person who has written to you, but could also be to an editor of a newspaper or the manager of a company, for example. It is important that you identify who you are writing to before you start your response. It is also important to decide on the register, and to write your email or letter in an appropriate way for the recipient.

There is one letter and one email task included in the examples in this book, with one being more formal and the other more informal (see pages 25 and 33).

Task type 4: Proposal

A proposal is written in response to a request for ideas from either a peer group, such as members of a club, or a superior, such as a college principal or work supervisor. They may also be written in response to a wider call for feedback on plans – for example, following an announcement of funding for a project and requests for ideas on how to use the money. It is often useful to include headings in proposals so that the different sections are clearly set out. Language should be persuasive but polite, and proposals are semi-formal in register.

Task type 5: Report

A report is usually written for a teacher or school principal, or a specific group such as the members of a club of society to which you belong. Reports are mostly factual and need to be based on the situation that is presented in the question.

Reports at this level go beyond those at B2 level, which are mostly descriptive. At C1, you need to show that you can evaluate the information and use this to, for example, suggest an alternative course of action or to say if an aim has been achieved.

Reports are typically semi-formal and often contain more impersonal language, such as passive forms. As with proposals, headings can help to show the different sections of your report.

Task type 6: Review

A review may be about a book, film, play, show or concert, but could also be about a product (for example, a kitchen gadget), or a service, such as a tour of a museum. You will be asked to give your opinion, but at this level you will also need to evaluate the subject of the report for a particular group of people or reason. The target reader will be described in the question, and you should make sure that you write your report with them in mind.

Reviews often include a range of different adjectives and, at C1, also include language of justifying opinions.

How to use this book

The main section of this book focuses on each task type individually, explaining its characteristics and providing guidance on how to plan a response to an example question.

For each task-type question, two responses from different students are provided. One response is very good and the other is less good, identifying areas that the student could improve on.

There are detailed comments on each response, and a breakdown of the marks that

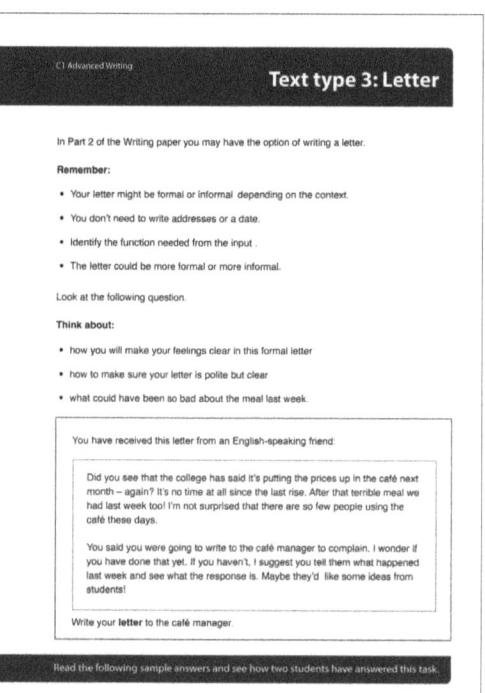

Introduction

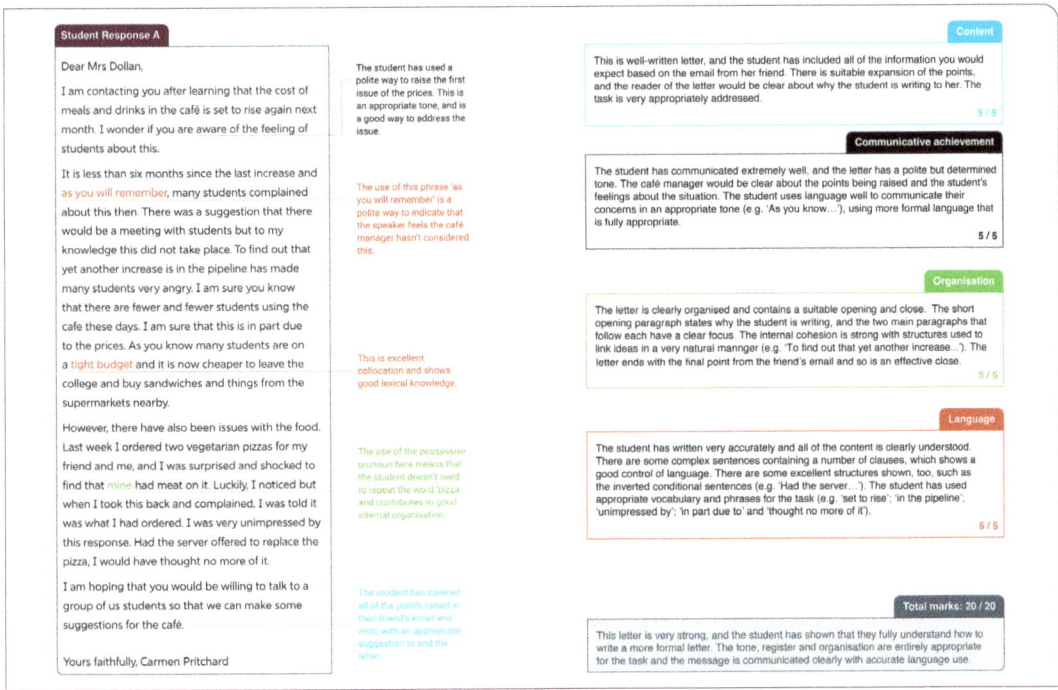

the response could get in the exam. You should read these responses and commentary before you write your own response to the question.

When you have written your response, look back at the comments and the mark scheme, and think about what you did well and also how you could have done better.

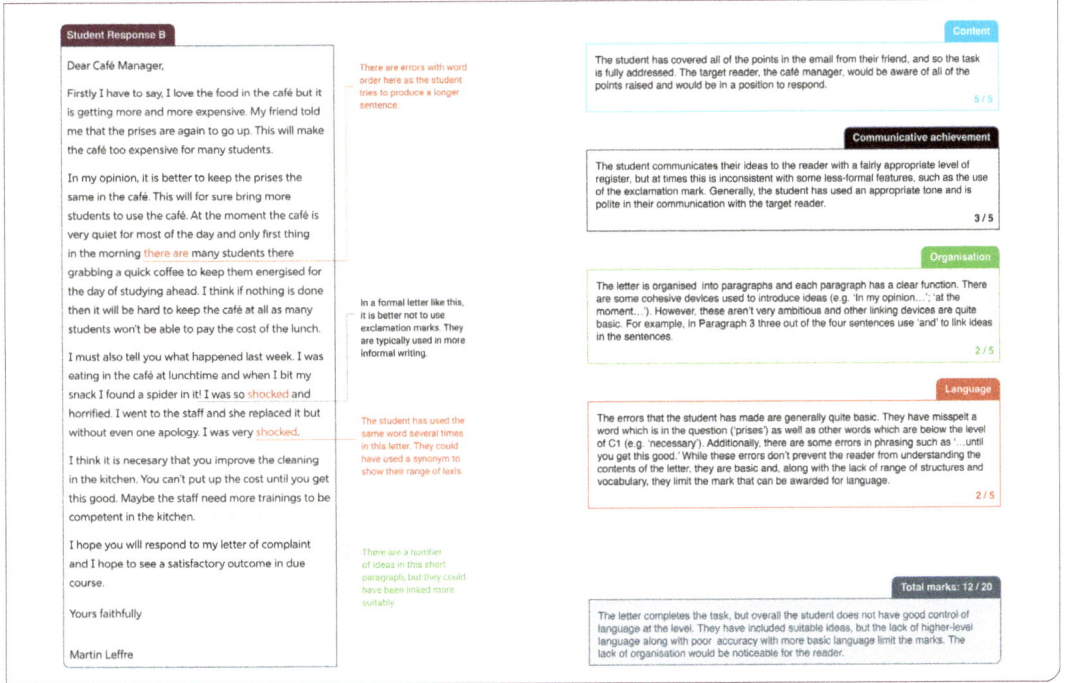

Preparing for the exam

It is important that you plan your time in the exam. You will need to complete both tasks within the 90 minutes. It is sensible to divide your time equally between the two tasks: about 45 minutes each. You should make sure that you:

- **Read** all of the questions carefully to be certain you understand what they mean.
- **Plan** your writing.
- **Write** your response according to your plan.
- **Check** your writing for errors.

Read the questions

Read the Part 1 question carefully, and identify the two ideas that you want to focus on in your essay. Read all of the Part 2 questions. There will be three questions, and you will need to choose one. When making your choice, you will need to think about the task type, the topic and the language that you will need. For example, there may be a question with a letter to be written relating to a concert. If you know lots of high-level vocabulary relating to music and the arts, then this could be a good choice. Another question might be a proposal about how to use some funding for a project in the community. If you feel that organisation of your writing isn't your strength, then choosing such a question might help as you can define the paragraphs by each funding idea. It is good advice to spend time thinking about each question before you start writing. If you start one question and then realise that you don't feel confident about the ideas or language you need, you may need to change question.

Plan your writing

It is tempting to start writing as soon as you decide what question to answer, but spending some time planning is very sensible. Students plan their writing in different ways, but the following is an example of a plan for the review response for the question on page 57:

> Intro: long-awaited show 'The Magician' | posters around town | stars on TV recently | Is it worth it?
>
> Para 1: story well known | took a dislike | actor fantastic | character so arrogant | getting more and more angry | infuriating | happy ending not believable
>
> Para 2: All is all?? | I recommend it | keep silly storyline in mind | lighting & special effects out of this world | made tricks seem real | you won't be disappointed in that
>
> Concl: Grab your ticket now!

Here, the candidate has noted down some ideas and good vocabulary to use, and has decided what will go in each paragraph.

Write your response

Use your notes to assemble your ideas from your plan into a well-organised piece of writing with a suitable tone and good, accurate language. With good planning technique, this will be easier. Of course, you will also be thinking about the functions, grammar and vocabulary that you considered before you started to produce your plan. This is the best way to make sure that you show the examiner as much of your language ability as possible.

It is a useful skill to paraphrase language that you find in the task. So, if the task says 'Have you seen a show at the theatre recently where you disliked the main character?', you could answer by saying 'I saw a show where I disliked the main character...'. But it would be better to paraphrase and say something like 'I really couldn't stand the leading character in a musical I watched the other day...'.

What language do you need?

There are three things to consider when you have read the questions. There is some overlap between them, but it is still a good idea to think about all three.

1. What functions does the task need?

For example, do you need to make a suggestion, evaluate something or justify a decision?

2. What grammar can you use in the task?

This may be linked to the functions of the question. For example, if you are asked to give or justify a decision, you can use the infinitive to show purpose and cohesive devices like 'due to this' or 'as a result of…'. Sometimes the grammar you use will be your choice. If you know that you are confident when using complex conditional sentences, can you include one in your response? If you know that you don't feel confident about using relative clauses, how can you avoid trying to use one and show some other impressive language instead?

3. What vocabulary is related to the task topic and links in with the functions?

If you are giving recommendations in the task (for instance, maybe in a report), you should think about what phrases you can use to make sure that there is variety. For example, it is better not to start each idea with 'I think…'. You could use 'One perspective I have considered…' or 'It cannot be denied that…' as alternatives to make sure that you show the examiner a good range of different phrases.

Check your writing

You should always leave five minutes to read through each response you write. Check that you haven't left anything important out, but also check the language for errors.

For example:

- *Have you used the right tenses?*
- *Have you used linking devices?*
- *Are there any spelling errors?*

It's a good idea to make your own checklist while you prepare for the C1 Advanced Writing paper. It will help you to think about what to check for, and also to think about mistakes that you often make.

Here is a suggested checklist to use, but it's a good idea to add things that you know you sometimes make mistakes with.

What would you add to this checklist?

✓ ✗

- [ ] Does your response cover all of the content points in the task?
- [ ] Is your response in the right style for the task type?
- [ ] Have you used the right register for the task?
- [ ] Have you used paragraphs to separate different ideas?
- [ ] Have you used linking devices correctly?
- [ ] Have you got a range of linking devices?
- [ ] Are all tenses correct?
- [ ] Have you used articles with nouns where needed?
- [ ] Are the prepositions correct?
- [ ] What about errors you've made in the past?

The assessment criteria

Each piece of writing is marked against four assessment criteria, each carrying a maximum of five marks.

Content

This criterion focuses on whether you have answered the question and whether the reader would have all the information they need. You must make sure that you identify what the question is asking you to do and plan your answer so that you stay on the topic. In Part 1 you must cover two ideas from the question, make a choice from them and give reasons for your choice. In Part 2 questions you must identify what you will need to write about from the question.

Max. 5 marks

Communicative achievement

This criterion focuses on how well you communicate with the reader. This includes whether your writing is suitable for the task you are writing and that it also involves register. Register means whether your writing is more formal (e.g. writing for someone you don't know) or less formal (e.g. writing for your classmates).

Max. 5 marks

Organisation

This criterion focuses on how your ideas are organised into paragraphs, if these are needed. It includes the use of discourse markers (e.g. 'and', 'but', 'so' at a basic level; and 'therefore', 'despite this' at a higher level). It also includes things like how pronouns are used to refer to nouns to avoid repetition. For example: 'He never liked school and hated going there...'. In this sentence 'there' means that the student doesn't repeat the word 'school'.

Max. 5 marks

Language

This criterion focuses on vocabulary and grammar. It isn't just about using vocabulary and grammar without making mistakes. It also considers whether your writing uses more difficult grammar and more unusual words and phrases. It is sometimes hard to focus on both, and, of course, it's great if you don't make any mistakes! However, if this means that your language is very simple, it may mean that you can't get to the top marks here.

Max. 5 marks

When all four criteria have been assessed your total mark is given out of 20.

Planning Guide

Write the question you are going to answer below, and underline or highlight the important words that will help you to focus your response.

What **functions** does the task need?

What **grammar** could you use?

What **vocabulary** could you use?

Bring your ideas together in a plan, and think about the organisation and register you need.

- How many paragraphs do you need? How will you link ideas?
- Who is your reader? What is your relationship to them?
- Do you need to use more formal or more informal language?

Text type 1: Essay

C1 Advanced Writing

In Part 1 of the Writing paper you will have to write an essay. **Remember:**

- Include two points or ideas from the question material.
- Make sure that you support your opinion with other points and reasons.
- Write a plan to organise your ideas into a well-thought-out argument.
- Bring your ideas together in a clear conclusion.

Look at the following question. **Think about:**

- how you imagine you would feel about doing voluntary work
- What areas volunteers might get involved in
- The pros and cons of each point made.

Your class has listened to a radio discussion about the value of young people doing voluntary work in the community. You have made the notes below:

Benefits of voluntary work:
- Meet different people
- Gain work experience
- Contribute to society

Some opinions expressed in the discussion:

"It might be a good thing if you don't have lots of friends!"

"A good idea for young people to gain work experience but what about the cost?"

"I'm sure it must feel really satisfying to have done your bit and contributed to something which helps people."

Write an essay discussing **two** of the benefits of voluntary work. You should **explain what the most significant benefit** of voluntary work is, **giving reasons** in support of your answer.

You may, if you wish, make use of the opinions expressed in the discussion, but you should use your own words as far as possible.

Read the following sample answers and see how two students have answered this task.

Student Response A

In recent times the idea of volunteering has become more and more popular. There are various benefits to volunteering, but also some downsides.

This is a straightforward introduction that clearly sets out what the essay is going to be about.

While I agree that it's a positive thing to have on your CV when you apply for jobs, it isn't always a straightforward thing. It may depend on what the voluntary work is, and how well organised it is of course. If there isn't a good structure to it, then it is possible that the volunteers will not gain as much as they wanted. In fact, they may be seen as a replacement for a member of staff in some situations. This should not happen.

This short sentence makes the student's point strongly and is very effective.

Doing volunteering in some place like a hospital, where you can help the sick with things like getting things from a shop and maybe reading to the old people would seem a very good idea though. This shows an employer that you have skills to get on with people and are compassionate. I think any employer would see this as a plus point.

The language used is generally very accurate and there is some good vocabulary used, like 'compassionate'.

However, the most important benefit of volunteering is that society benefits as a whole. The skill of helping others makes you into a good citizen who knows that it is important to look at the situation of others as well as your own. In these days when young people in particular are often told they are selfish, this must be seen to be the greatest benefit.

The student has covered two ideas from the question, but not very evenly. They wrote about the idea of getting work experience at great length and so may have run out of time, and words, for the second point. Nevertheless, this is a strong essay.

Content

The essay covers two of the bullet point areas indicated in the task: gaining work experience and the benefit to wider society. The student has drawn on the comments in the task but has also included their own ideas. They have fully addressed the task requirements.

5 / 5

Communicative achievement

The tone and register of the essay are entirely appropriate, and the student has considered the target reader in their writing. The essay ends slightly suddenly with the answer to the final part of the task about what the more important point is. With a slightly stronger conclusion this would have achieved the full 5 marks.

4 / 5

Organisation

The essay is well organised with a short but relevant introduction to lead into the main part of the essay. The student has used cohesive devices with flexibility to introduce ideas (e.g. 'while I agree…', 'In fact…') and has made use of referencing and elision to make the writing flow well.

4 / 5

Language

The grammar used in the essay is very accurate. There are some complex sentences with a number of clauses. The student has used a conditional form, modal verbs and a relative clause with good control but could have shown a wider range of language. There is some good vocabulary used which is relevant to the task (e.g. 'downside', 'straightforward', 'a plus point', 'citizen').

4 / 5

Total marks: 17 / 20

Overall, this is a strong essay that fully addresses the task and communicates with the target reader well. The student has expanded on some of the points in the task and has included their own opinion.

Student Response B

Thinking of doing voluntary work? Well...

...really you should! In my experiences, the best thing about volunteers is that they learn a lot of new skills and this is useful in your career in the future.

For some people the best thing is to work in the industry or job that you want to work. You can maybe contact a big company and see if they need an intern. This will mean that you work alongside the other people in the company and learn direct from them. This is very valuable and you may make some contacts to get a paid work there later.

At a minimum, you should learn from this experience what it is like to work in this company. Is it a good fit for you later? Maybe you will find from doing this that the job you think you wanted isn't so good. You won't waste a lot of time apply for this job in this case.

For some people, they maybe get some money to pay for their travel to the company and their lunch maybe. You shouldn't expect this though and you maybe have to work without money for a few months as an intern.

But all in all, it is the best way to discover your true job ambitions. I think the idea of doing voluntary work in a company and learn about work skills is very precious. Do it!

The student has approached this essay more like an article. The heading would be good for an article but not an essay. The tone throughout isn't appropriate for an essay.

The student has misinterpreted the focus of the essay, and, although they started well, the essay starts to move away from the focus of volunteering here.

There is some confusion with the use of tenses here.

The student uses the same word 'maybe' a number of times in this paragraph. Remember to try to vary the language you use to show a range.

Text type 1: Essay

Content

The student has started to write about doing voluntary work, but has slightly misinterpreted the focus of the task. They have focused on being an intern instead of doing voluntary work in a wider sense, and so have missed the opportunity to use the bullet points given to expand on the topic well. This has limited the development of the task.

3 / 5

Communicative achievement

The student has written the essay to sound more like an article, with a heading and matching closing comment. This doesn't communicate well and the tone and register they have used are not suitable for a semi-formal essay. They have also made their writing more informal by referring to 'you' a number of times (e.g. 'You can maybe contact…', 'you should learn from…'). Essays are usually less direct in their referencing.

2 / 5

Organisation

The essay is organised and has clear paragraphs. The last paragraph is also introduced by a suitable phrase to sum up ideas (e.g. 'But all in all…'). In some places in the essay the student has used more basic connecting devices and could have shown a range of different ways to make the essay flow well.

3 / 5

Language

The student has made some more basic errors in their writing (e.g. '…get a paid work…'). There is some lack of control of tenses as well. There are some instances where the phrasing doesn't read very naturally, but overall the meaning can always be understood. However, the language the student has used in fairly simple and doesn't quite reach the level required for C1.

2 / 5

Total marks: 10 / 20

The task has not been fully understood by the student and by producing an article style they have not written appropriately for the target reader – their teacher. Their writing moves slightly away from the focus of the task by concentrating on working for a company rather than volunteering in a wider sense. The student's range of language is not at the appropriate level for C1, despite the fact that all of the essay can be understood.

C1 Writing | Cambridge Masterclass

Now have a go at writing a response to this question yourself.

Your class has listened to a radio discussion about the value of young people doing voluntary work in the community. You have made the notes below:

Benefits of voluntary work:
- Meet different people
- Gain work experience
- Contribute to society

Some opinions expressed in the discussion:

"It might be a good thing if you don't have lots of friends!"

"A good idea for young people to gain work experience but what about the cost?"

"I'm sure it must feel really satisfying to have done your bit and contributed to something which helps people."

Write an essay discussing **two** of the benefits of voluntary work. You should **explain what the most significant benefit** of voluntary work is, **giving reasons** in support of your answer.

You may, if you wish, make use of the opinions expressed in the discussion, but you should use your own words as far as possible.

Highlight or underline the important words.

Outline plan:

Refer to the Planning Guide on page 14 for guidance on how to plan your response.

Text type 1: Essay

Write your response (220–260 words).

✔	✘	
☐		Does your response cover all of the content points in the task?
☐		Is your response in the right style for the task type?
☐		Have you used the right register for the task?
☐		Have you used paragraphs to separate different ideas?
☐		Have you used linking devices correctly?
☐		Have you got a range of linking devices?
☐		Are all tenses correct?
☐		Have you used articles with nouns where needed?
☐		Are the prepositions correct?
☐		What about errors you've made in the past?

Text type 2: Email

C1 Advanced Writing

In Part 2 of the Writing paper you may have the option of writing an email.

Remember:

- Make sure that you cover the content points in the task.
- Identify the functions required in the task.
- Write with an appropriate register for the reader.
- Use a suitable opening and close.

Look at the following question.

Think about:

- what structures you can use for giving advice
- language relating to art and exhibitions
- whether you will recommend visiting the gallery or not.

Read part of an email from a friend who is planning to visit an art exhibition that you saw recently.

> I heard that you went to the exhibition at the National Art Gallery last week. I am hoping to go soon but it's very hard to get tickets. It's been very popular! How did you get your tickets?
>
> Sara said that you had some other problems too. Is that right?
> I'm wondering if it's worth going now. What do you think?

Write your **email**.

Read the following sample answers and see how two students have answered this task.

C1 Writing | Cambridge Masterclass

Student Response A

Hi James.

It's good to hear from you after so long. When I was having lunch with Sara on Friday, she mentioned that she was hoping to catch up with you at the weekend.

This is a good introduction to the email. It sets the tone well, but isn't too long.

You're right – getting tickets was a headache but I don't think it's because there are lots of people want to go. The website is very hard to book on. It crashed many times when I was buying my ticket. I was very keen to see the exhibition. As you know it is my favourite artist. Why don't you go to the gallery to buy your ticket there? I should have done that! It must be easier.

The internal organisation here could be better – the student could have joined these two sentences.

The exhibition is amazing. I really recommend getting to it if you can. There aren't that many pictures but they are wonderful! The artist is very different as it is modern art and some people there didn't understand it. I heard some people complaining that it wasn't proper art and that they regretted coming and paying so much for their tickets. I think the tickets are cheaper with a student discount card, so don't forget to take your ID with you! If I didn't have so much to do for my exams next month, I would come with you again! That's a recommendation, isn't it?

This is a nice informal phrase and is used very naturally here. It's better than just saying 'going to it'.

Let me know what you think of it. Maybe we can have a coffee and catch up soon.

Maria.

There is good paragraphing with the two main points in the email split into the 2nd and 3rd paragraphs.

Text type 2: Email

Content

The student has shown a clear understanding of the task requirements. They have written about the problem with getting tickets in an appropriate manner and have included another issue. These points have been incorporated into a well-written email.

5 / 5

Communicative achievement

The communication is entirely appropriate in this email. As the email is to a friend, it is informal, and the language used reflects this. The opening is friendly and sets the scene for communicating effectively and naturally with the reader. The student uses language well in Paragraph 3 to communicate her enthusiasm for the exhibition, and this reads very clearly.

5 / 5

Organisation

The email is well-organised and has an appropriate opening and close for an informal email. The content is divided into suitable paragraphs, and there is good referencing to the email the student has received (e.g. at the start of Paragraph 2: 'You're right — …'). Some of the sentences are quite short, and the student could have used cohesive devices to link these. Despite this, the organisation is strong.

4 / 5

Language

The language used is appropriate to the task, and the student has written very accurately. There is a good range of structure, such as the use of the past continuous in the first paragraph (e.g. 'When I was having…'; 'She was hoping…'), and there are some complex sentences (e.g. in Paragraph 3: 'I heard some people…for their tickets'). There is occasional good vocabulary use (e.g. 'crashed' referring to the website), but this could have been more ambitious.

4 / 5

Total marks: 18 / 20

This is a strong response to the task and the student has written a very natural email using language that is suitable for the target reader. Their friend would be fully informed as all content is relevant to the questions asked in their email. The student has good control of language and writes very accurately.

Student Response B

Hey Carla,

Thank you for your email and I was very happy to receive your news.

I can tell you all about the art exhibition but I did have some issues when I went to the gallery. I think it is a good exhibition but on the other hand it was very busy. It isn't cheap either, so you should go at the end of the day, when it is more cheaper, I think.

There were many laws at the gallery and I couldn't take in my drink what I have just brought. I had to drink it very quick outside, and I had an arguement with the ticket office about this. I think they should tell you that this isn't possible, before.

The man in the office was very rude.

The exhibition wasn't very good. It was too difficult to see the pictures, and I could go right close to them, as the crowds of people didn't move. The gallery staff needed to be more in control of this, so that all people can see everything.

Also, you can't take big bags in the gallery. They tell you to go to the station to leave big bags in the luggage counter. I had my work case with me and I couldn't go in with it. There are a lot of things to remember before you go!

The pictures were so so. Not very good, and not very bad. But in conclusion, I think it is better to look at it all on the internet. And it's cheaper!

See you soon, Marco

The student has opened with an informal greeting, which is suitable for this reply to a friend but the first line of the email sounds more formal, which makes it slightly inconsistent.

There are a lot of paragraphs in this email, and this one in particular is very short. The student would have benefited from considering this more when they planned their writing.

The email covers a number of different issues at the gallery, but jumps around a lot. The student might have been better to focus more on fewer problems.

This is good informal language, but it isn't used with very complex grammar.

Content

The student has answered the email they received, and has presented a number of problems they encountered. They haven't specified how they got their tickets for the exhibition, though, so the task isn't fully addressed. They may have benefited from including fewer other issues and expanding on them more. However, they have raised a problem other than getting tickets, so this part of the requirements has been met.

4 / 5

Communicative achievement

The register of the email is generally informal with a friendly greeting ('Hey Carla!'), which is suitable for an email to a friend. However, the opening paragraph is rather more formal and some other phrases are also more formal (e.g. 'But in conclusion…' in the last paragraph). The email doesn't communicate very clearly, partly because so many ideas are presented too briefly.

2 / 5

Organisation

The organisation of the email is not strong. There are too many paragraphs and one paragraph of only one sentence. The ideas in the email are confused, and the student has used simple cohesive devices for the internal organisation. The ideas within the email are all relevant but needed better organisation to present them more logically.

2 / 5

Language

The student uses a narrow range and has not shown a control of language required for this level. There are some examples of basic errors in language use (e.g. 'more cheaper', 'all people can see everything'). On occasion these make the meaning unclear (e.g. 'It was too difficult to see the pictures, and I could go right close to them, as the crowds of people didn't move.'). Additionally, there is some incorrect vocabulary used (e.g. 'laws' rather than 'rules' in Paragraph 3).

2 / 5

Total marks: 10 / 20

Although the student has understood the task and has generally produced appropriate content, they have not demonstrated a suitable range of language and show some inaccuracy. The email is difficult to read due to the poor internal organisation and some language errors. The student has not reached the level required for C1.

Now have a go at writing a response to this question yourself.

Read part of an email from a friend who is planning to visit an art exhibition that you saw recently.

> I heard that you went to the exhibition at the National Art Gallery last week. I am hoping to go soon but it's very hard to get tickets. It's been very popular! How did you get your tickets?
>
> Sara said that you had some other problems too. Is that right?
> I'm wondering if it's worth going now. What do you think?

Write your **email**.

Highlight or underline the important words.

Outline plan:

Refer to the Planning Guide on page 14 for guidance on how to plan your response.

Text type 2: Email

Write your response (220–260 words).

✓	✗	
		Does your response cover all of the content points in the task?
		Is your response in the right style for the task type?
		Have you used the right register for the task?
		Have you used paragraphs to separate different ideas?
		Have you used linking devices correctly?
		Have you got a range of linking devices?
		Are all tenses correct?
		Have you used articles with nouns where needed?
		Are the prepositions correct?
		What about errors you've made in the past?

Text type 3: Letter

C1 Advanced Writing

In Part 2 of the Writing paper you may have the option of writing a letter.

Remember:

- Your letter might be formal or informal depending on the context.
- You don't need to write addresses or a date.
- Identify the function needed from the input.
- The letter could be more formal or more informal.

Look at the following question.

Think about:

- how you will make your feelings clear in this formal letter
- how to make sure your letter is polite but clear
- what could have been so bad about the meal last week.

You have received this letter from an English-speaking friend:

> Did you see that the college has said it's putting the prices up in the café next month – again? It's no time at all since the last rise. After that terrible meal we had last week too! I'm not surprised that there are so few people using the café these days.
>
> You said you were going to write to the café manager to complain. I wonder if you have done that yet. If you haven't, I suggest you tell them what happened last week and see what the response is. Maybe they'd like some ideas from students!

Write your **letter** to the café manager.

Read the following sample answers and see how two students have answered this task.

33

Student Response A

Dear Mrs Dollan,

I am contacting you after learning that the cost of meals and drinks in the café is set to rise again next month. I wonder if you are aware of the feeling of students about this.

It is less than six months since the last increase and as you will remember, many students complained about this then. There was a suggestion that there would be a meeting with students but to my knowledge this did not take place. To find out that yet another increase is in the pipeline has made many students very angry. I am sure you know that there are fewer and fewer students using the cafe these days. I am sure that this is in part due to the prices. As you know many students are on a tight budget and it is now cheaper to leave the college and buy sandwiches and things from the supermarkets nearby.

However, there have also been issues with the food. Last week I ordered two vegetarian pizzas for my friend and me, and I was surprised and shocked to find that mine had meat on it. Luckily, I noticed but when I took this back and complained, I was told it was what I had ordered. I was very unimpressed by this response. Had the server offered to replace the pizza, I would have thought no more of it.

I am hoping that you would be willing to talk to a group of us students so that we can make some suggestions for the café.

Yours faithfully, Carmen Pritchard

The student has used a polite way to raise the first issue of the prices. This is an appropriate tone, and is a good way to address the issue.

The use of this phrase 'as you will remember' is a polite way to indicate that the speaker feels the café manager hasn't considered this.

This is excellent collocation and shows good lexical knowledge.

The use of the possessive pronoun here means that the student doesn't need to repeat the word 'pizza' and contributes to good internal organisation.

The student has covered all of the points raised in their friend's email and ends with an appropriate suggestion to end the letter.

Text type 3: Letter

Content

This is well-written letter, and the student has included all of the information you would expect based on the email from her friend. There is suitable expansion of the points, and the reader of the letter would be clear about why the student is writing to her. The task is very appropriately addressed.

5 / 5

Communicative achievement

The student has communicated extremely well, and the letter has a polite but determined tone. The café manager would be clear about the points being raised and the student's feelings about the situation. The student uses language well to communicate their concerns in an appropriate tone (e.g. 'As you know…'), using more formal language that is fully appropriate.

5 / 5

Organisation

The letter is clearly organised and contains a suitable opening and close. The short opening paragraph states why the student is writing, and the two main paragraphs that follow each have a clear focus. The internal cohesion is strong with structures used to link ideas in a very natural manner (e.g. 'To find out that yet another increase…'). The letter ends with the final point from the friend's email and so is an effective close.

5 / 5

Language

The student has written very accurately and all of the content is clearly understood. There are some complex sentences containing a number of clauses, which shows a good control of language. There are some excellent structures shown, such as the inverted conditional sentences (e.g. 'Had the server…'). The student has used appropriate vocabulary and phrases for the task (e.g. 'set to rise'; 'in the pipeline'; 'unimpressed by'; 'in part due to'; and 'thought no more of it').

5 / 5

Total marks: 20 / 20

This letter is very strong, and the student has shown that they fully understand how to write a more formal letter. The tone, register and organisation are entirely appropriate for the task and the message is communicated clearly with accurate language use.

C1 Writing | Cambridge Masterclass

Student Response B

Dear Café Manager,

Firstly I have to say, I love the food in the café but it is getting more and more expensive. My friend told me that the prises are again to go up. This will make the café too expensive for many students.

In my opinion, it is better to keep the prises the same in the café. This will for sure bring more students to use the café. At the moment the café is very quiet for most of the day and only first thing in the morning there are many students there grabbing a quick coffee to keep them energised for the day of studying ahead. I think if nothing is done then it will be hard to keep the café at all as many students won't be able to pay the cost of the lunch.

I must also tell you what happened last week. I was eating in the café at lunchtime and when I bit my snack I found a spider in it! I was so shocked and horrified. I went to the staff and she replaced it but without even one apology. I was very shocked.

I think it is necesary that you improve the cleaning in the kitchen. You can't put up the cost until you get this good. Maybe the staff need more trainings to be competent in the kitchen.

I hope you will respond to my letter of complaint and I hope to see a satisfactory outcome in due course.

Yours faithfully

Martin Leffre

There are errors with word order here as the student tries to produce a longer sentence.

In a formal letter like this, it is better not to use exclamation marks. They are typically used in more informal writing.

The student has used the same word several times in this letter. They could have used a synonym to show their range of lexis.

There are a number of ideas in this short paragraph, but they could have been linked more suitably.

Text type 3: Letter

Content

The student has covered all of the points in the email from their friend, and so the task is fully addressed. The target reader, the café manager, would be aware of all of the points raised and would be in a position to respond.

5 / 5

Communicative achievement

The student communicates their ideas to the reader with a fairly appropriate level of register, but at times this is inconsistent with some less-formal features, such as the use of the exclamation mark. Generally, the student has used an appropriate tone and is polite in their communication with the target reader.

3 / 5

Organisation

The letter is organised into paragraphs and each paragraph has a clear function. There are some cohesive devices used to introduce ideas (e.g. 'In my opinion…'; 'at the moment…'). However, these aren't very ambitious and other linking devices are quite basic. For example, in Paragraph 3 three out of the four sentences use 'and' to link ideas in the sentences.

2 / 5

Language

The errors that the student has made are generally quite basic. They have misspelt a word which is in the question ('prises') as well as other words which are below the level of C1 (e.g. 'necessary'). Additionally, there are some errors in phrasing such as '…until you get this good'. While these errors don't prevent the reader from understanding the contents of the letter, they are basic and, along with the lack of range of structures and vocabulary, they limit the mark that can be awarded for language.

2 / 5

Total marks: 12 / 20

The letter completes the task, but overall the student does not have good control of language at the level. They have included suitable ideas, but the lack of higher-level language along with poor accuracy with more basic language limit the marks. The lack of organisation would be noticeable for the reader.

C1 Writing | Cambridge Masterclass

Now have a go at writing a response to this question yourself.

You have received this letter from an English-speaking friend:

> Did you see that the college has said it's putting the prices up in the café next month – again? It's no time at all since the last rise. After that terrible meal we had last week too! I'm not surprised that there are so few people using the café these days.
>
> You said you were going to write to the café manager to complain. I wonder if you have done that yet. If you haven't, I suggest you tell them what happened last week and see what the response is. Maybe they'd like some ideas from students!

Write your **letter** to the café manager.

Highlight or underline the important words.

Outline plan:

Refer to the Planning Guide on page 14 for guidance on how to plan your response.

Text type 3: Letter

Write your response (220–260 words).

✔	✘	
		Does your response cover all of the content points in the task?
		Is your response in the right style for the task type?
		Have you used the right register for the task?
		Have you used paragraphs to separate different ideas?
		Have you used linking devices correctly?
		Have you got a range of linking devices?
		Are all tenses correct?
		Have you used articles with nouns where needed?
		Are the prepositions correct?
		What about errors you've made in the past?

C1 Advanced Writing

Text type 4: Proposal

In Part 2 of the Writing paper you may have the option of writing a proposal.

Remember:

- A proposal is written to a person in authority.
- It is different from a report in that it looks forward to future action.
- The use of passive forms is common in proposals.
- Proposals usually require different options to be considered and a recommendation given.

Look at the following question.

Think about:

- how you will use the content points to structure your proposal
- what might worry people about such a large event
- what your recommendation would be to deal with local concerns.

You see this announcement in an English-language magazine for young people:

> There are plans to hold a large sporting event in your region. You feel that the town would be a good location for it. You decide to write a proposal for the town council saying why the sporting event should come to the town, how the event would benefit local people and what concerns local people may have.

Write your **proposal**.

Read the following sample answers and see how two students have answered this task.

Student Response A

I write with regard to the National Youth Games which are to be held in the north of the country. I would like to propose our town as a suitable venue and hope that the town council will support this. This proposal will set up the details for this suitability and the potential benefits to the town. I would like to bring to your attention the facilities which we have in the town. By this I refer to not only the sporting areas in the town, but also the world class hotels and restaurants.

The sports included in the National Youth Games can take place in existing facilities which are located in the same part of town. This will be efficient and more economical to provide staff. The athletic stadium in particular has experience of these kind of events as in 2020 an international event was held there and this was highly successful.

Some local people are worried about the lack of facilities, but I believe they are not aware of how well-eqiped the town has become. We have five star hotels with superb facilities. These are suitable for not only the sportsmen and women, but also the many thousands of visitors who would come to watch events. It would be advisable to inform local residents about this to encourage them to accept this proposal. As the town has an aim of being a green town, a green approach to the event should be encouraged.

I believe this is an outstanding opportunity for the town and hope that you will be in agreement with me.

The student has used passive forms like this one in a number of places in their proposal. This helps to make the response more impersonal.

Phrases like 'I would like to bring to your attention...' help to set the tone for the proposal and communicate effectively.

There is repetition of the same word here. It is better to try to use a synonym or to rephrase.

The student has used a more complex structure here ('not only...but also...') to join ideas.

Although all content from the question is covered, this last point does not link very well and makes this paragraph less cohesive.

Content

The student has included all of the required content in their proposal. They have expanded on the first point relating to how the town is equipped for the event very well. Although the second point about any local concerns is not covered in as much depth, it is included and so the reader would be fully informed.

5 / 5

Communicative achievement

A suitable tone is used and more formal language is included in the proposal (e.g. 'I write with regard…'). This is appropriate for a proposal to a town council. The language choice helps to establish a professional and objective tone to the proposal that communicates well with the reader.

4 / 5

Organisation

The student has not used headings for the proposal, but it is still well-organised. Paragraphing is suitable and the proposal ends with a strong closing sentence to conclude. There is suitable use of cohesive devises to join ideas in the proposal (e.g. 'By this…'). These are sometimes repeated as with the structure 'not only…but also'. This is still strong organisation, but with more variety the student might have achieved full marks for this criterion.

4 / 5

Language

The language used in the proposal is strong and the student has written accurately in general. Errors are minor, such as the spelling mistake with 'eqiped' and the incorrect participle with the multi-word verb 'set up the details'. The vocabulary used is suitable for the topic and the task type (e.g. 'I would like to propose…'; 'superb facilities'; 'a green approach').

4 / 5

Total marks: 17 / 20

This is a strong proposal and it is written in a suitable tone. The student has a good understanding of the task type and has used language that aims to be detached and more formal. They have organised their ideas well and the writing is generally accurate. The target reader would be fully informed.

Student Response B

Dear Head of sports,

I am writing to support the bid for the town holding the International Athletics Championships in our town. I strongly feel we have the right characteristics and it would be highly beneficial for our area. I hope you agree to bring your championships to the town.

Facilities: We have a wonderful stadium in our town which is rarely used. It has the possibility to provide a suitable venue for the championships. I am confident that with a little work, it could be ready for use in time. After talking to the management, they have requested a small amount of money to paint some corridors and halls. This would be a good investment and would ensure that the stadium is ready for the world to see. This work would take 2 weeks approx.

Visitors: As you know the town needs investment and local people are worried about this and this would be a great opportunity to entice a large number of visitors to the town. The shops and restaurants would be happy to have extra custumers and there would be more money made by local people if there were lots of visitors.

Relaxing: We have plenty of places for visitors to relax in the town and our parks can be available for them to relax at the end of the sporting day. We can use this to attract more visitors in the future too.

I propose we hold a meeting in the near future to ensure we can secure this fantastic opportunity!

Your faithfully, Jane Turner

The opening greeting is not needed here as this is a proposal and not a letter.

The student has used headings to organise their report.

This should have been written in full. Try not to use abbreviations in more formal writing.

Although this isn't an error, the two uses of 'this' here make the sentence awkward to read. The sentence could have been reworded to avoid the repetition.

The tone of the proposal is not sufficiently formal in places, and the register is inconsistent.

Text type 4: Proposal

Content

The reader of the proposal has been misunderstood, and the student has written to the person making the decision about the location of the event rather than to the town council. The student has included a significant amount of information about the suitability of the town for holding the event. However, they have not included any information about the concerns of the people in the town, and so the proposal is only partially complete and the target reader would not be fully informed.

3 / 5

Communicative achievement

The communicative achievement of this answer is mixed. The student mostly uses a formal register, but the use of the inclusive pronoun 'we' at times confuses the reader as the student talks about bringing 'your championships to the town'. This confusion stems from the misinterpretation of the target reader. The use of a letter layout is not appropriate to a proposal. Despite some very relevant communication, the reader would be confused.

2 / 5

Organisation

There is suitable organisation of the writing, with paragraphs used clearly and headings to show what each paragraph refers to. There is some suitable internal cohesion with phrases such as 'After talking to the management…' and referencing like '…we can use this…'. At other times linking is more simple.

3 / 5

Language

The level of grammar is mixed, with some usage being at C1 level and some slightly below. Although there are few errors, the student has not been ambitious and tried to use a range of different structures. For example, 'It has the possibility to provide a suitable venue for the championships...' could have been phrased as 'With some adaptations the venue would be the perfect location for the event...'. There is some vocabulary that raises the level of the writing (e.g. 'highly beneficial'; 'support the bid'; 'entice'). The vocabulary choice is stronger than the structure in this proposal.

3 / 5

Total marks: 11 / 20

The task type has been confused here and the target reader would not be fully informed. There is a lack of grammar at the appropriate level, and, despite the lack of errors, this alone limits the marks the student can be awarded. The organisation is the weakest area, and the candidate would have benefitted from considering how to link ideas within the proposal more clearly.

Now have a go at writing a response to this question yourself.

You see this announcement in an English-language magazine for young people:

> There are plans to hold a large sporting event in your region. You feel that the town would be a good location for it. You decide to write a proposal for the town council saying why the sporting event should come to the town, how the event would benefit local people and what concerns local people may have.

Write your **proposal**.

Highlight or underline the important words.

Outline plan:

Refer to the Planning Guide on page 14 for guidance on how to plan your response.

Text type 4: Proposal

Write your response (220–260 words).

✔	✘	
☐		Does your response cover all of the content points in the task?
☐		Is your response in the right style for the task type?
☐		Have you used the right register for the task?
☐		Have you used paragraphs to separate different ideas?
☐		Have you used linking devices correctly?
☐		Have you got a range of linking devices?
☐		Are all tenses correct?
☐		Have you used articles with nouns where needed?
☐		Are the prepositions correct?
☐		What about errors you've made in the past?

C1 Advanced Writing

Text type 5: Report

In Part 2 of the Writing paper you may have the option of writing a report.

Remember:

- A report looks back and reflects on a past event.
- At this level, you will be expected to evaluate rather than just describe.
- There are likely to be recommendations for change or improvement.
- A title and subheadings will help you to organise your report.

Look at the following question.

Think about:

- the type of charity the website might be for – this may provide some subject-specific vocabulary
- what you usually look for on websites and what could be useful for users of a charity website to know about
- what could be lacking from a website based on your experience
- how to make suggestions linked to the idea of making the website more attractive
- what makes a website more attractive. Think about websites that you like using, and some that aren't as user-friendly.

You work for a small charity which is planning to update its website.

You have been asked to write a report about the website by your manager and to include your ideas about how to make the charity more appealing to young people, suggestions for getting more visitors to the site and how to get any changes made.

Write your **report**.

Read the following sample answers and see how two students have answered this task.

Student Response A

WEBSITE DEVELOPMENT: A REPORT

Introduction: The purpose of this report is to provide feedback on the current website design and to make suggestions for consideration in its development. A survey of users was conducted to inform the findings of this report and these users acted as a focus group.

Feedback: The most common view was that the website is generally clear and well laid out. However, 40% of those surveyed stated that the website looked very similar to another charitys site and this is a concern that should be addressed as a priority.

Potential improvements: Furthermore, having colours on the site that were brighter could not only differentiate it from other similar sites, but act as a link to the other activities we carry out. When this suggestion was put before a sample of users it was reported that this would make it distinctive.

Links to the youth market: In order to make best use of the website, and to make the whole work of the charity more relevant to younger people, some articles showing how the local college students have worked with us could help to connect with a younger audience.

Conclusion: I believe we have the necessary expertise in the charity to make these changes. With some simple changes, our website can become a leader in the field and will help all of us to draw more attention to our important work.

This is a simple but clear heading. Report headings should be factual and don't need to be exciting to catch the eye as the reader has requested the report and so plans to read it.

This is one approach to a report: to base it on a survey. This provides scope to report on the results or what participants have said.

The student has missed the apostrophe here. Be sure to check your work for punctuation.

The report has good internal organisation as the student has used phrases like 'in order to' to show their intentions.

Text type 5: Report

Content

The rationale for writing the report has been clearly understood, and the student has included all the points required by the question. They have used an approach of having carried out a survey to inform the content and this is one approach to report writing which may be useful. The content is full and the student has expanded on each point.

5 / 5

Communicative achievement

The student has communicated very effectively. They have used an appropriate tone and the report uses formal language. The language is impersonal and precise, and this helps the reader to understand the content.

5 / 5

Organisation

There is a factual heading and sub-headings that link to the points in the question. These help the student to organise their writing clearly. The student has used some formal cohesive devices to introduce ideas in the report (e.g. 'however'; 'furthermore'). There is also effective referencing (e.g. 'when this suggestion…'), which means that the report reads very naturally.

5 / 5

Language

Both structure and vocabulary are used effectively in the report, and there is a very high level of accuracy. The student has chosen structures suitable to a report – for example, the passive with a modal verb ('should be considered') and participle clauses ('having colours'). The vocabulary is also suitable for the task, and there is some excellent collocation (e.g. 'with ease'; 'differentiate it from'; 'tasked with'). Apart from a minor error with punctuation, the report is highly accurate.

5 / 5

Total marks: 20 / 20

This report demonstrates the student's excellent control of language use in all areas. They have fully understood the task and have produced a detailed report that would fully inform the target reader. The appropriate organisation and natural use of language fully completes the task.

Student Response B

Report on charity website

Introduction: This report is about the company I work for which is a charity. The work of the charity is very important and due to this, it is important to make the website appealing and open to all people.

It isn't necessary to state all of the information included in the question. Here, the student has said that they work for the charity, but, as the report has been requested by their manager, this isn't needed.

Website improvements: The website at the moment is quite good but it could be improved. I believe the best websites should have clear menus so that people can find things easily. A good menu is essential for users, with drop downs so that it is quick and simple to find information about the charity. In addition to this, I think we could add a button so that people can give money to the charity.

The student has used some good vocabulary linked to websites, menu, drop downs, etc., but it is quite basic.

Making the website wider known: The charity should make the website better known so that everyone knows about the charity. This will be good for our clients. We could advertise the charity more clearly and with wider advertising. If you include the link to the website on all of this it will help in this. In addition, add a QR code. Most young people will prefer this.

The student has used referencing well here to avoid repeating the word 'advertising'.

Cost: All in all, the cost of making the improvements to the website is about £1000. As it is a charity, it may be possible to get some donations from companies to do this changes.

Conclusion: To sum up, the work to the website in very important and should be done as soon as possible to make it more appealing to the young people and good for the charity.

Although the student makes an attempt at writing more formally, the report has a number of instances of phrases such as 'I think...' and 'we could...'. The student could have used less personal structures to make the report more formal.

Text type 5: Report

Content

The task has been attempted well, and the student has included a range of information about how to make the website better. They have not fully addressed the point about getting young people more involved through the website, and so the target reader would not be fully informed. The student has also misinterpreted the point about getting the changes made.

4 / 5

Communicative achievement

Generally, the student has communicated their ideas clearly in their report. The introduction is not necessary, and this could confuse the reader as this is shared information in this context. The language is occasionally more personal than it should be for a report (e.g. 'I think we could add…'; '…if you include…'). In other places, however, the candidate uses more appropriate language (e.g. 'A good menu is essential for users…').

3 / 5

Organisation

The organisation of the report includes headings for each paragraph, and, although some of these are general (e.g. 'Making the website wider known'), they are suitable topics for each paragraph and show overall organisation. There is some good use of cohesive devices (e.g. '…due to this…'; 'All in all…' and 'to sum up'). They have also used referencing to aid organisation.

4 / 5

Language

The student writes accurately in some places, but the language used is limited in range. Despite some relevant vocabulary for talking about websites (e.g. 'menu'; 'drop down'), the structures used are quite simple. For example, the student uses modal verbs often and would have benefited from showing alternative language. Overall, despite the lack of serious errors the report lacks the range of language required for C1.

2 / 5

Total marks: 13 / 20

The student has not fully addressed all of the task requirements, but the report has some good features and the organisation is a strength. However, the language used is often fairly simple, and, despite the good vocabulary, overall it is below the level required at C1.

C1 Writing | Cambridge Masterclass

> **Now have a go at writing a response to this question yourself.**

You work for a small charity which is planning to update its website.

You have been asked to write a report about the website by your manager and to include your ideas about how to make the charity more appealing to young people, suggestions for getting more visitors to the site and how to get any changes made.

Write your **report**.

> **Underline the important words.**

Outline plan:

> **Refer to the Planning Guide on page 14 for guidance on how to plan your response.**

Text type 5: Report

Write your response (220–260 words).

✔	✘	
		Does your response cover all of the content points in the task?
		Is your response in the right style for the task type?
		Have you used the right register for the task?
		Have you used paragraphs to separate different ideas?
		Have you used linking devices correctly?
		Have you got a range of linking devices?
		Are all tenses correct?
		Have you used articles with nouns where needed?
		Are the prepositions correct?
		What about errors you've made in the past?

Text type 6: Review

C1 Advanced Writing

In Part 2 of the Writing paper you may have the option of writing a review.

Remember:

- A review could be of a book, performance, service or item.
- The target reader will be specified, and you should consider this in your writing.
- Good reviews will include a range of adjectives.
- An evaluation is required, not just a description.

Look at the following question.

Think about:

- how the characters are important to a show
- why you might dislike a character
- what might make up for disliking a character.

You see the following announcement on a theatre website called GREAT SHOWS:

> **REVIEWS WANTED!**
>
> Have you seen a show at the theatre recently where you disliked the main character?
>
> Why did you not like the character? Did it have an impact on your enjoyment of the whole show?
>
> Tell us whether you would still recommend the show.
>
> The best reviews will be published next month.

Write your **review**.

Read the following sample answers and see how two students have answered this task.

Student Response A

Grab a ticket!

Last week I went to see the long-awaited show 'The Trick' at the Opera House. I'm sure you have seen all of the posters about it around town, and the stars were on TV recently advertising it. But is it worth splashing out on tickets?

It can't be denied that the story is well known, so there are no surprises there. But pretty soon, I took a dislike to one of the characters: the magician's son. The actor is fantastic, and very well known from his TV work, and I can't say anything bad about his acting but really, he was so arrogant. I found myself getting more and more angry with him. The way he talked to the other people in the show was infuriating. Of course, the show has a happy ending but I really didn't find it believable. How can there be such a change in someone's behaviours due to one little accident? I won't tell you more and spoil it for you!

So, all in all, what do I recommend? Well, despite this I say go and see it but keep in mind that you have to try to keep calm and forget the silly storyline. The lighting and special effects are out of this world! It's worth the money to see that anyway. I was amazed at how they used the lighting to make the magician's tricks seem real. That was more impressing than the annoying magician's son. If you focus on that and forget the character, then I am sure you won't be disappointed. Grab your ticket now!

The student has used a short heading to introduce the review, and this gives us an immediate idea of the content and attracts the reader.

This is good vocabulary to use, and the student has correctly used a hyphen for the compound adjective. This shows the examiner that they understand the use of more complex adjectives.

Good skills in collocation are shown here with the phrase 'take a dislike'.

This phrase indicates that a conclusion is coming but links back to the content of the previous paragraph well.

The student has cleverly mirrored their heading in the closing phrase, and this rounds the review off well with a suitable tone.

Text type 6: Review

Content

The review describes one of the characters in a show, but the student hasn't stated that this is the main character. However, this is a minor slip and apart from this the content is clear and relevant to the question set, and the review gives relevant information about the impact that their dislike for the character has overall.

5 / 5

Communicative achievement

The tone of the review is entirely appropriate; the language is used effectively to communicate ideas to the reader and it has a consistent register. The student has used devices such as rhetorical questions to engage the reader. The language used is lively and helps to make the review interesting to read.

5 / 5

Organisation

There is effective organisation of the review with three paragraphs that each have a clear function. The student uses cohesive devices well (e.g. 'despite this…' and 'on balance'). The use of rhetorical questions is effective in introducing a new paragraph (e.g. 'But is it worth splashing out on tickets?'), and structures are used well to show links with different ideas.

5 / 5

Language

The language in the report is highly accurate, and the student has demonstrated a wide range, both of structure and vocabulary. There are examples of different tenses (e.g. 'you will have seen'; 'the stars have been…') and structures such as the conditional form. The vocabulary used is particularly effective (e.g. 'long-awaited'; 'splashing out'; 'infuriating'; 'keep calm'). Along with the wide range of language used, the student has written highly accurately.

5 / 5

Total marks: 20 / 20

Despite the error in not identifying the chosen character as the main one, the review is very strong. The language use is natural and has been well considered. The student has organised the review well, and the tone is entirely appropriate for a review.

Student Response B

Theater review

I am writing this review to enlighten you on a show I saw recently. It was really amazing and I think everyone should go see it without any delay. I had gotten my ticket from a friend and I wasn't too excited about it really. Fairly soon, I changed my mind and I think you should too! It's sure to be a sell out so don't delay!

ACTING: I have been inclined to see this show for the longest time frame. Disillusionment approached though! The acting wasn't so good. Maybe the nastiest I have seen in a protracted time. But the main character isn't sympethetic. His wife in the show is a newcomer. However, in spite of this, her acting is broadly of a suitable standard.

SCENARY: This was very simple and I think it could be better if more things were available for the actors to use during the show. This was a significant disadvantage of the show. In other shows I saw recently the scenery played a more active part and it was quiet eccentric. Morover, they should have been considering this more.

TICKETS: The ticket's cost wasn't too much and didn't break the bank. It was really quite good value and I can recommend you buy one.

SUMMARY: Overall, in my opinion I think I can sum up to say that it was good value. The show is going to be at the capitol theatre until July 30th and there are plenty of tickets for each day. But maybe think twice if you want a good experience.

The student has used American English in many places in this review ('theater'; 'I had gotten…'). This is acceptable, but you should be consistent with language choice.

The opening title is rather dull and isn't likely to attract readers to the review, but the student has used suitable sub-headings and they all relate to theatre. However, the paragraphs are very short and so it might have been better to focus more on developing each paragraph.

Most of the review is descriptive, and there isn't much evaluation. Remember that, at C1 level, reviews move on from just describing.

The student hasn't covered all of the points in the task, and so the content is not complete.

Text type 6: Review

Content

The task is attempted, and the target reader is on the whole informed. Much of the content of the review is general, but in the question an actor is identified for comment. However, the recommendation is slightly confused as the student is generally positive about the show but ends with a slightly negative statement.

3 / 5

Communicative achievement

The communication is slightly confused as the start of the review reads slightly like a letter rather than a review. The tone is mixed, with some content being fairly informal and suitable for a review and other content presented with some more formal language, particularly some of the cohesive devices, such as 'moreover' (spelt 'morover' by the student).

2 / 5

Organisation

There is an attempt at suitable paragraphing, but there are a lot of paragraphs and some don't relate directly to the question. The student has used cohesive devices, but these are often used inappropriately (e.g. 'Morover, they should…' and 'Despite this…'). In other places simple connectors are used – for example, two sentences are connected with 'and' in Paragraph 3.

2 / 5

Language

Some of the language is in American English (e.g. 'I had gotten…' and '…should go see it…'). This is acceptable, but its use must be consistent throughout the writing. There is a lot of more ambitious lexis in the review, but this is mostly used inappropriately (e.g. '…to enlighten you on a show…') and the student lacks control of this language. In some cases, more basic structures and vocabulary are not used totally accurately, and the student has not shown flexibility in their use of this language.

2 / 5

Total marks: 9 / 20

The review is fairly general and could have been more closely focused on the task. The student has been ambitious in their use of language, but does not show good understanding of choice of vocabulary. This results in a very mixed tone that makes the communication of ideas difficult to follow in places. Along with the misuse of some cohesive devices, this means that the review does not reach the required standard for C1.

C1 Writing | Cambridge Masterclass

Now have a go at writing a response to this question yourself.

You see the following announcement on a theatre website called GREAT SHOWS:

REVIEWS WANTED!

Have you seen a show at the theatre recently where you disliked the main character?

Why did you not like the character? Did it have an impact on your enjoyment of the whole show?

Tell us whether you would still recommend the show.

The best reviews will be published next month.

Write your **review**.

Underline the important words.

Outline plan:

Refer to the Planning Guide on page 14 for guidance on how to plan your response.

Text type 6: Review

Write your response (220–260 words).

C1 Writing | Cambridge Masterclass

✓ ✗

☐ Does your response cover all of the content points in the task?

☐ Is your response in the right style for the task type?

☐ Have you used the right register for the task?

☐ Have you used paragraphs to separate different ideas?

☐ Have you used linking devices correctly?

☐ Have you got a range of linking devices?

☐ Are all tenses correct?

☐ Have you used articles with nouns where needed?

☐ Are the prepositions correct?

☐ What about errors you've made in the past?

Practice tests

Test 1 | p.67

Question	Task type
1	essay
2	proposal
3	letter
4	report

Test 2 | p.77

Question	Task type
1	essay
2	proposal
3	review
4	email

Test 3 | p.87

Question	Task type
1	essay
2	review
3	report
4	proposal

Test 4 | p.97

Question	Task type
1	essay
2	report
3	email
4	review

Cambridge C1 Advanced Writing

Practice test 1

Part 1

You must answer this question. Write your answer in 220–260 words on the answer sheet.

Question 1

Your class has taken part in an online debate about participation in organised sport by young people.

You have made the notes below:

Benefits of being active:

- Learn to work as a team
- Ensures good work/life balance
- Encourages a healhy lifestyle

Some opinions expressed in the discussion:

"Being in a team means people get competitive, which I hate."

"After a long day of study, I don't have the energy to go and play football."

"I feel so much less stressed when I find time for a class at the gym, but a walk outside is just as beneficial."

Write an essay discussing **two** of the benefits of being active. You should **explain which one is the most achievable for young people**, giving reasons in support of your answer.

You may, if you wish, make use of the opinions expressed in the discussion, but you should use your own words as far as possible.

Planning page

Answer sheet

Question 1

Answer sheet

Continued

Part 2

Write a response to one of the questions 2–4. Write your answer in 220–260 words in an appropriate style on the answer sheet.

---

2. Your college has been given a grant from the regional art gallery and your principal would like to use it to make your college building more attractive for students. You have been asked to produce a proposal suggesting how the money could be spent, both inside the college and in the grounds. You should include information about how this will be of benefit to student life.

    Write your **proposal**.

3. You are reading your local newspaper and find a letter criticising young people for using social media.

    > It's such a pity to see young people always on social media these days. They don't realise how much of the real world they are missing out on!
    >
    > David Collins
    >
    > To give YOUR view, contact the editor by writing to Tom Mallard.

    Write your **letter** to the editor of the newspaper giving your views.

4. Your town recently ran a scheme to encourage people to buy things locally to support local businesses. As a member of the youth council, you have been asked to write a report about how well the scheme achieved its aims. You have been asked to include feedback from local businesses to support your report.

    Write your **report**.

Planning page

Answer sheet

Question ☐

Answer sheet

Continued

Cambridge C1 Advanced Writing

Practice test 2

Part 1

You must answer this question. Write your answer in 220–260 words on the answer sheet.

Question 1

Your college recently attended a seminar called 'Access to the Arts', which focuses on how this is important for young people.

You have made the notes below:

Benefits of having access to the Arts:

- Provides different experiences
- Inspires creativity
- Benefits other areas of life

Some opinions expressed in the discussion:

"The schemes which make it cheaper for young people to go to theatres, shows and galleries are great – I wish there were more."

"I think of some of the amazing things I've seen and know that I could never achieve that."

"I've read that in countries where children study the arts more, they do better in subjects like maths and science. I wonder if there's a link."

Write an essay discussing **two** of the benefits of having access to the arts. You should **explain which one is the most significant benefit of having access to the arts**, giving reasons in support of your answer.

You may, if you wish, make use of the opinions expressed in the discussion, but you should use your own words as far as possible.

Planning page

Answer sheet

Question 1

Answer sheet

Continued

Part 2

Write a response to one of the questions 2–4. Write your answer in 220–260 words in an appropriate style on the answer sheet.

---

2   You see this announcement on your town website about your local train station and decide to write a proposal with suggestions saying how different people could benefit from the additional facilities.

> Following feedback in recent years about the lack of facilities at the train station, we are delighted to inform you that we have received permission to expand. We would be pleased to receive proposals with ideas on how we should use the additional area to serve all of our users.

Write your **proposal**.

3   You and your family recently took a city bus tour in a tourist destination you visited and have decided to write a review of the tour. You should include information on what you enjoyed and what could be improved, as well as saying whether the tour was suitable for children.

Write your **review**.

4   You see this announcement in your local sports centre:

> **NOTICE TO MEMBERS**
> From next month there will be some exciting changes at the centre!
> - You will be able to use the pool to hold children's parties in the evenings – you can use the website to book.
> - We are improving the café area and will have an increased menu. Please see the café menu for our new prices.
> - Our classes are very popular and we have decided to make a small charge for booking these in advance. This will mean you are sure of a spot!
> We hope you will enjoy these improvements!
> Kate Jenkinson (Manager)

You decide to email the manager of the centre giving your views on the changes. Write your **email**.

Planning page

Answer sheet

Question ☐

Answer sheet

Continued

Cambridge C1 Advanced Writing

Practice test 3

Part 1

You must answer this question. Write your answer in 220–260 words on the answer sheet.

Question 1

Your class has taken part in an online debate about flexible working, where people work from home sometimes.

You have made the notes below:

Features of flexible working:

- Staff are often more productive working from home
- More effective communication via email and chat groups
- Helps the environment by cutting down on commuting

Some opinions expressed in the discussion:

"Some days I get a lot done, but on other days I get distracted if my flatmates are at home."

"It's so lonely working at home – I miss seeing my colleagues."

"The amount of time and money I save on not travelling into the office is amazing."

Write an essay discussing **two** of the features of flexible working. You should **explain which one is the most advantageous feature**, giving reasons in support of your answer.

You may, if you wish, make use of the opinions expressed in the discussion, but you should use your own words as far as possible.

Planning page

Answer sheet

Question 1

Answer sheet

Continued

Part 2

Write a response to one of the questions 2–4. Write your answer in 220–260 words in an appropriate style on the answer sheet.

---

2 You see this announcement on an entertainment website: LEISURE TODAY.

> **Reviews wanted!**
>
> This month we are doing something different! We are looking for reviews of books which have been made into films.
>
> Were the book and film the same?
>
> Did you watch the film first or read the book?
>
> And, of course, which was better?
>
> We will publish the best reviews next month.

Write your **review**.

3 You came to study at your college from abroad and have now been asked by the college principal to write a report about the support provided to international students. You should include what was beneficial to you as well as any areas that the college may not have considered previously.

Write your **report**.

4 Your town has decided to close a large car park near the centre of town that isn't used much and to use it for something else. You decide to write a proposal saying how best to use the land to allow different sections of the community to benefit, while keeping costs down.

Write your **proposal**.

Planning page

Answer sheet

Question ☐

Answer sheet

Continued

Cambridge C1 Advanced Writing

Practice test 4

Part 1

You must answer this question. Write your answer in 220–260 words on the answer sheet.

Question 1

Your class has taken part in a debate about access to the internet.

You have made the notes below:

Features of access to the internet:

- Convenient for consumers
- Saves time on daily tasks
- Easy contact

Some opinions expressed in the discussion:

"Some of the things advertised online are just rubbish! And you don't know until they arrive."

"I can't believe my parents used to queue up at a bank to pay bills – what a waste of time and energy."

"People assume everyone has access to a device to get online to chat – it's not the same for everyone and some people are being left behind."

Write an essay discussing **two** of the features of access to the internet. You should **explain which is the most widespread benefit of this access**, giving reasons in support of your answer.

You may, if you wish, make use of the opinions expressed in the discussion, but you should use your own words as far as possible.

Planning page

Answer sheet

Question 1

Answer sheet

Continued

Part 2

Write a response to one of the questions 2–4. Write your answer in 220–260 words in an appropriate style on the answer sheet.

---

2   The company you work for provides catering facilities for its staff to use as well as areas for relaxing. You have been asked to write a report on how these facilities are used by staff and which facilities they value the most. You should include in your report suggestions for how they could be improved to increase their use.

   Write your **report**.

3   You have received this email from your English friend:

   > Hi there!
   >
   > I'm emailing to see if you can help me and my friends. As you know I'm a member of an amateur drama club and we desperately need to raise some funds for our next show. We've tried the usual things and have another cake sale this weekend. But we need to do more! Do you have ideas of things we can try? Or do you know anyone who might be willing to sponsor us? If we don't raise money soon, we may have to cancel the show! Help!
   >
   > Angela

   Write your **email**.

4   A sports website has asked you to write a review of a sporting event which you attended recently, saying why you decided to attend the event and which aspects of it you thought were particularly successful. You should also include at least one thing that you think could have been better.

   Write your **review**.

Planning page

Answer sheet

Question ☐

Answer sheet

Continued

www.ingramcontent.com/pod-product-compliance
Lightning Source LLC
Chambersburg PA
CBHW051316110526
44590CB00031B/4377